Singing
★ ★ ★ ★ ★
A PRACTICAL GUIDE TO PURSUING THE ART
★ ★ ★ ★ ★

BY REBECCA LOVE FISHKIN

CONTENT ADVISER
Andrea Leap, Voice Instructor,
MacPhail Center for Music

READING ADVISER
Alexa L. Sandmann, EdD, Professor of Literacy,
College and Graduate School of Education, Health, and Human Services,
Kent State University

COMPASS POINT BOOKS
a capstone imprint

Compass Point Books
151 Good Counsel Drive
P.O. Box 669
Mankato, MN 56002-0669
877-845-8392
www.capstonepub.com

Editor: Jennifer Fretland VanVoorst
Designer: Ashlee Suker
Media Researcher: Svetlana Zhurkin
Library Consultant: Kathleen Baxter
Production Specialist: Jane Klenk

Image Credits
Alamy: B. O'Kane, 35, David J. Green, 6, Imagebroker, 5, Jeff Greenberg, 43, Jim West,
15, 27, Martyn Vickery, 40, Richard Levine, 19, Simon Price, 26; Compass Point
Books, 12; Ed Livernoche, 24; Getty Images: AFP/Janek Skarzynski, 22, Bloomberg/
Gregorio Marrero, 9, Ethan Miller, 38, Michael Becker, 31, Wireimage/Jeffrey Mayer,
32, Workbook Stock/Zave Smith, cover; iStockphoto: Anna Lubovedskaya, 36,
Mikhail Tolstoy, 4, Pali Rao, 44, Reuben Schulz, 21; Shutterstock: Adam Fraise, 16,
Ferenc Szelepcsenyi, 20, Jason Stitt, 34, Lisa F. Young, 7, Nicole Weiss, 17, Ronald
Sumners, back cover (background texture) and throughout, Tracy Whiteside, 28,
Voyagerix, 11, William Attard McCarthy, 45; Svetlana Zhurkin, 37.

Library of Congress Cataloging-in-Publication Data
Fishkin, Rebecca, 1972–
    Singing : a practical guide to pursuing the art / by Rebecca Love Fishkin.
       p. cm. — (The performing arts)
    Includes bibliographical references and index.
    ISBN 978-0-7565-4362-4 (library binding)
    1. Singing—Vocational guidance—Juvenile literature. I. Title.
    II. Series.
    ML3795.F546 2011
    783—dc22   2010012607

Printed in the United States of America in Stevens Point, Wisconsin.
022011   006100R

TABLE OF CONTENTS

You're a Singer

Since ancient times people have raised their voices in song to celebrate, communicate, mourn, pray, and remember. Singers are storytellers, using their voices to share a message. From a mother's soft lullaby to a global concert, song brings people together.

The human voice may have been the first musical instrument. Ancient people used their voices—and later, flutes, drums, and other instruments—to imitate the

Classical singers perform music from opera, a kind of musical play.

sounds of nature. Ancient Egyptians used music as part of their religious ceremonies. The Greeks later used music as entertainment. As Christianity grew, monks sang simple, single-line chants that would become the foundations of classical music. Musicians began to combine multiple musical parts. Then they added voice.

Music spread to the masses. Singers called minstrels wandered Europe, telling musical stories. Kings hired singers and held public concerts. Opera houses opened. The invention of recording devices made music available to most of the world. Today almost anyone can hear songs using radio, television, recordings, or the Internet.

Singing differs among countries, regions, and even states. In the United States, people listen to rock and roll, pop, blues, jazz, folk, country, opera, rap, hip-hop, gospel, world music, and more. The choices are seemingly limitless, and the possibilities of what you can *do* with song are endless.

You can sing hymns in church or show tunes in a play. You can sing a cappella or with instrumental accompaniment. You can make albums and radio jingles. You can sing on Broadway, at weddings, and at hospitals.

You are a singer, but what does that mean? What stories do you want to share, and how do you want to tell them? More important, do you know how to use your tools— your voice, your body, your determination, and your creativity—to get to where you want to go?

Many famous singers began by singing into a hairbrush in front of a mirror.

Chapter 1

The Basics of Singing

A singing sound occurs when air passes over the vocal cords and causes them to vibrate. Physically, however, singing involves much more than that. Before you can become a successful singer, you must learn about:

Breathing

Voice

Rhythm

Listening

To build a strong, pleasing singing voice, you must understand each element and how it works in harmony with the others.

Breathing

Breath control is the foundation of singing. Without it, no other skill can be mastered. A singer must breathe using the diaphragm. This means controlling your abdominal muscles so your breath feels as if it were going in and out of your stomach, not your chest.

Inhale deeply and slowly through your nose. Let the breath fill your abdomen first and then rise through your chest to your throat. Exhale from your chest to your belly, then out. Practice inhaling to the count of five, holding for five, and then exhaling for five. Keep your stomach relaxed.

Try this: Lie on your back and place several heavy books on your stomach. Slowly breathe in and out,

Scream It!

Have you ever really listened to a heavy-metal singer scream? It is not as easy as it sounds. Learning a proper rock scream is a great way to learn to use your diaphragm. A rock scream should come from your belly, not your throat. It should not strain your voice.

making the books rise and fall. Now sing in this position. Watch how the books move. With practice, you should be able to control the weight and balance of the books while smoothly singing a whole song.

Just as important as breathing correctly is *remembering* to breathe while singing. Do not hold your breath while you hold notes. Learn how long you can hold a note on a breath and where you need to take breaks. Make your inhalations part of the song, not pauses in it. Try to do this quietly. The last thing a listener wants to hear is loud breathing.

Opera legend Mirella Freni shows a student how breath support can help singers reach the high notes.

Now stand straight. Posture is part of breath and voice control. Keep your gaze at eye level. Tilting your chin up or down can compress your vocal muscles. Relax your shoulders and place your feet flat on the floor. Practice your stance until you feel relaxed and comfortable. Open your mouth wide to sing, but do not force your jaw. Your tongue should be relaxed.

Voice

Once you learn to control your breath and your body, you can improve your voice to find a richer, broader sound. This means working on pitch and voice register.

Pitch is how high or low the sound is when you sing a note. When your pitch is correct, your singing voice sounds in tune with the rest of the music.

To recognize proper pitch, play a note on a tuned piano. Then sing the note aloud. Does your voice sound the same as the piano? Learning to hear and sing pitches accurately will do wonders for your singing. It will help you know when your songs are going well, and it will help you expand your voice range.

You may already know your voice range—soprano, alto, tenor, or bass. Your voice range is the notes you can sing, from your lowest note to your highest. Singers often struggle to stay on pitch as they strain to reach notes that

Having a piano handy when you sing will help you find the right pitches.

seem too high or low. Understanding what voice registers are can help you expand your comfort zone.

The voice changes as it resonates in various parts of the body. Each part is a different register. Voices can sing in three registers—a chest voice, a middle (or mixed) voice, and a head voice.

Your voice resonates along your pharynx, which is the area from your nasal cavity down through your larynx into your esophagus. Try sliding your voice up and down a scale of notes, from low to high to low by making an "ahh" sound. Listen to where your voice resonates. The highest sounds come from your nasal cavities (head voice), the middle sounds come from the back of your mouth

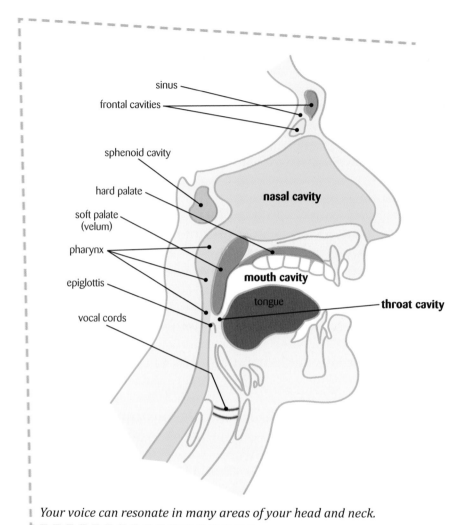

sinus

frontal cavities

sphenoid cavity

hard palate

soft palate
(velum)

pharynx

epiglottis

vocal cords

nasal cavity

mouth cavity

tongue

throat cavity

Your voice can resonate in many areas of your head and neck.

(middle voice), and the lowest sounds come from your

throat (chest voice).

With practice you can learn to hit the high and low notes

in your range more easily, and to move from note to note

more smoothly. Mastering your middle voice, however, will

result in your strongest sound, because it mixes the best

notes of your head and chest voices.

While working on your pitch and range, think about how you use your voice to shape sounds and words. Have you ever listened to a song without understanding a word? Diction—correct, clear pronunciation—is important to making

Do, Re, Mi

In the musical *The Sound of Music*, Maria, the governess, teaches the von Trapp children to sing scales using the syllables "do, re, mi, fa, so, la, ti, do." Try singing one syllable on one note for as long as you can. Do not strain your breath, throat, or stomach. Then do the other sounds with different notes.

a song pleasant to hear, and to making the words clear. Do not mumble or exaggerate. You must learn proper enunciation to make your words sing. If your audience cannot understand your story, they will not connect with you.

Rhythm

Songs move to a tempo—a beat—that sets the pace and mood. Think about dancing. The faster the rhythm, the faster you want to move. And slow songs make for slow dances.

WARM-UP EXERCISES

Athletes warm up and cool down before a game or practice. Singers, too, need to care for their voices and bodies. Some simple warm-up and cool-down exercises can help keep your voice in top condition.

You can find free singing exercises online. Before starting, talk to your voice instructor, music teacher, or another singer to see what exercises are right for you and to make sure you are properly following the directions.

Breathing: To warm up your diaphragm, take a deep breath to "fill" your belly. Slowly exhale while making a constant sound (such as "sssss"). Use your breath and tongue to keep the sound and volume steady. Repeat a few times. Next, make the same sound loudly while you exhale quickly and dramatically. The sound will be forceful. Repeat. Last, make and stop the sound many times during one exhalation. It should sound fast and light. Repeat.

Neck and shoulder stretches: Gently lean your right ear to your right shoulder and hold for a moment. Repeat on the left. Do not strain your muscles. Let them relax. Hunch your right shoulder toward your right ear, hold for a moment, and then release. Repeat on the left. Then do both shoulders at once. Turn your head gently toward the right, and then back to the left several times. Keep your jaw relaxed.

Singers with the Mosaic Youth Theater warm up before a rehearsal.

Tongue exercises: Open your mouth and wag your tongue around. Press it against your teeth and then to the roof of your mouth. Curl it backward. Then curl the sides upward.

Lip trilling: Pretend to blow bubbles under water. Relax your lips and let them vibrate steadily as you exhale. Then try it while voicing one note.

Scales: First hum scales, and then sing them. Start with short ones. Sing up and down a scale. Start low and work up to higher notes as your voice warms up. Sing scales using short notes, then longer notes.

A metronome ticks in time, helping you keep the beat.

When you sing, you must keep time with the rhythm of the song. If you sing too fast, the music will lag behind and sound out of sync. If you sing too slowly, you will have to rush your voice to catch up. Can you sing a song and keep the beat by tapping your foot?

Listen to your favorite songs. Do the music and voices work together? Listen to one song performed in different ways by various artists. How do they use rhythm to change the feel of the words?

Reading music can help you understand rhythm. Playing an instrument can help you improve even further and add another dimension to your performances.

Listening

Your voice is not your only singing tool. You need your ears as well.

Record yourself singing a song that you believe you sing well. Listen to it several times. Are you in tune? Is your breathing natural or too noticeable? Are you in tempo? Do you *like* what you hear?

Listen to how other singers combine voice and rhythm to impart meaning. How do they make an old song sound fresh? What vocal qualities attract you to your favorite singers? Your goal is not to copy them, but

Become a better listener, and you will become a better singer.

to analyze what you like and dislike, and then apply this knowledge to your own singing.

Listen when people give you feedback about your singing. It can be difficult to hear critiques, especially negative comments, but do not argue. Use it to improve. Most feedback can be helpful when you take some time to understand it.

Finally, listening is the best way to learn about a variety of song styles. Branch out from your favorites and listen to as many types of music as you can find. Go to concerts at theaters and schools. Download songs and make mixes. Experiment to find what works best with your voice and your style.

If your voice or throat feels strained, stop singing! But you need to take care of more than your voice. Drink plenty of water to stay hydrated. Aerobic exercise, such as swimming, increases lung capacity. Stretching activities, such as yoga, build strength and improve posture. Eat healthful foods, don't smoke, limit caffeine, and brush those teeth so you can show off your smile while you perform.

Music education is important. All musicians should learn about music theory and music history. You should learn about music styles, how to read music, and how your voice works. You will learn much of this in your school music courses, so take as many as you can.

To become a professional singer, however, you need to take that education out of the classroom and use it on stage.

One of the best ways to get singing and stage experience is to join a youth choir. This could be through a theater, place of worship, community center, or your school. Choirs

provide experience with various song styles, and you can be part of small, specialized groups within the larger choir or try out to be a soloist.

To experience performing in musical theater, join a drama club or try out for a school play. Call theaters to see whether they offer youth workshops, productions, camps, or summer programs. When you are older, you can work at a theater to learn about the business.

Your school music teachers are great first resources. Ask whether they offer summer courses or know of any good community singing programs.

Many places of worship offer opportunities to sing in a choir.

Musical theater is a fun way to perform as a singer while developing useful acting skills.

Look into programs at nearby colleges. Many colleges with music programs offer youth classes and camps. Community colleges may provide low-cost programs for area residents. And county and all-state choirs, as well as regional and national competitions, can expose you to new directors, travel, and stronger performance techniques.

Use the Internet to find singing opportunities. To make smart choices, read information carefully and print it or take notes. Never go to any programs or auditions, or sign up for any online programs, without an adult.

Do You Need a Voice Teacher?

Watch any music awards show, and you will hear the winners thank their grade-school music teachers for starting them on the path to success. For many singers, music education comes solely from school and stage experience. Others turn to voice teachers.

Private singing instructors offer classes and workshops, but individual lessons, though expensive, can be very helpful.

A personal voice teacher can help you maximize the potential of your voice.

Think about where you are getting your instruction now. Are you receiving enough personalized guidance? Do you think you need something more to reach the next level?

If you decide you want private lessons, make a list of nearby teachers from the phone book or the Internet. Ask your school music teacher or call college music or drama departments for recommendations. Ask other singers too.

Make appointments with several teachers. With an adult, meet each teacher to discuss your goals and current training. Ask about lesson plans and teaching techniques. Talk about cost and scheduling. Ask teachers about their backgrounds. How long have they been teaching? What kind of singing have they done and where?

Once you choose a teacher, respect his or her experience, and trust that the lessons are useful. Make sure that you, too, are respected. Your teacher should listen to your questions and concerns to create a program that meets your needs.

Amy Otey

Singing Fitness Instructor

Amy Otey did not set out to be a rock and roll star to the preschool crowd. Born in 1962, Otey was surrounded by music. Her mother played the piano, and her great-grandmother had played piano for silent pictures. Otey sang in the school choir and took part in musical theater productions. She considered studying music in college, but her mother encouraged her to sing as a hobby, not as a career. Otey earned a business degree and went to work as a resident services director for a retirement and nursing home. She also became a certified fitness instructor.

It was not until her son was born prematurely that singing became a focus of Otey's life. For three months, her only contact with her baby was to touch one of his fingers through his incubator in the hospital and to sing to him for hours. She began to realize the power of song. Her son's survival helped to give birth to a new career: Miss Amy, singer, songwriter, and music educator.

Otey began singing at libraries and parties. She became a certified music instructor. In 2004 she released her first CD, *Underwater*, and sang on the award-winning CD *International Baby 101*. Her fifth CD was released in 2010. Demand for Otey's shows grew, and she began performing for large audiences and on radio stations in Pennsylvania and New Jersey.

After performing and writing for years, Otey decided to take her music to a new level. Using her background as a yoga and fitness instructor, she created Miss Amy's Kids Fitness Rock & Roll Program. Her goals are to get children ages 2 to 8 to be physically active while listening to music, and to promote a lifelong appreciation of physical fitness. Using rock, folk, hip-hop, and other styles, Otey writes songs with patterns and instrumentation that appeal to children and parents. Otey also creates movement lesson plans for teachers and librarians on her Web site.

Otey still uses her voice to help sick children by volunteering with Musicians on Call, an organization that brings music to hospital patients. She also does volunteer performances for the Autism Society of America Foundation, the United Way of America, and the March of Dimes.

Otey tells young singers that being a good listener is just as important as singing: "There are performers and there are listeners. Learn to appreciate both and when to be which one."

The most important thing you can do to improve is to immerse yourself in music and to practice—all the time, Otey says. "Good song ideas are everywhere," she says. "Be a sponge. Seek out opportunities to experience as many different forms of music and singing as you can. Most of all, have fun. If you don't enjoy it, how do you expect your audience to?"

Chapter 3

What It Takes to Make It

Professional singers seem so sure of themselves on stage. Watch them move. The microphone looks as if it were part of their hands. They smile while singing big notes. They dance and sing without missing a beat or losing their breath.

What you do not see is what it takes to get there. Professional singing is a challenging career. Talent is simply not enough. To really make it in the music business, a singer must be determined. You have to want it, and it has to show. You need to work harder than ever before and bounce back from failures.

A good singer is willing to learn. Be versatile. Try new techniques and styles. Accept advice and criticism, and use it to your benefit. Learn when to ask for—and when to accept—help from others. Respect your teachers and peers. They have knowledge to share.

Singers need discipline. Practice, rehearsals, and performances are tiring and time consuming. You must develop stage presence—the ability to command the

Dress rehearsals are usually held the day before the performance. Singers re-create performance conditions by wearing performance dress and going through their entire program without pausing.

SINGING: A TEAM SPORT

"You may be a soloist, but you never sing on your own. Singing is a team sport—to succeed, you need good people skills," says singer and songwriter Amy Otey.

"You may be the one with the microphone, but unless the sound is right, the accompanist and you are on the same page, the lighting is pointed your way, the stage crew has set the stage, your dress or tie will not malfunction, and your makeup looks good, your performance will not reach its full potential. Divas are minimally tolerated by those good people around them."

audience's attention.

Beware of imitation. You may mimic a favorite singer beautifully, and this may even help you at first, because you sound like someone successful and popular. But do not get trapped. Find *your* voice. Originality is crucial.

It is easy to become discouraged by failed auditions and the difficulty of finding singing jobs. Persistence and optimism are your tools. Be confident in your voice and your goals, and keep trying.

Your big break might not look like anything you have ever dreamed about, so be ready to take whatever opportunities come your way.

Calm Down

To calm yourself before an audition or performance, Rock and Roll Hall of Fame singer Graham Nash says you need "a deep breath, knowledge that you want to share *your* work, then another deep breath."

PREPARING FOR AN AUDITION

Auditions are stressful, even for the most experienced singers. To help you prepare and relax:

» Know the audition rules. You may need to sing a particular type of music or part of a certain song. You may need your own sheet music and a résumé. Find out how long you will need to sing. Make sure you know the time and location of the audition.

» Choose a song you love. Learn those lyrics. Missing words will throw you off rhythm, and you may lose the job at once. An audition is the time to show your strengths, not to experiment. Choose a song that suits your voice and style.

» Get a good night's sleep before the audition. Dress appropriately. Arrive on time, or earlier. Bring water (and a snack if you expect a wait). Warm up thoroughly.

» When your name is called, take the stage with confidence. Find a comfortable stance. Breathe. Smile and make eye contact. Sing clearly and sincerely.

» Thank the reviewing panel when you finish, and be proud of yourself for completing the audition.

Be prepared for whatever happens by knowing that even your best performance may not land the spot. Your voice or appearance simply might not suit the role or position. Yet every audition is good experience. Use what you learn and keep trying.

Auditions can be scary, but have confidence in your ability and preparation. The more experience you have with auditions, the more comfortable with them you will become.

Graham Nash

Hall of Fame Superstar

One Sunday evening in England, when Graham Nash was a boy, he heard a radio broadcast of American rock and roll. It was the sounds of Elvis Presley, Buddy Holly, the Everly Brothers, Fats Domino, and Little Richard. Nash was hooked.

He formed a rock duo with a school friend, Allan Clarke, and they eventually teamed up with a few others to become The Hollies. Nash's voice was a cornerstone of the group's harmonious sound. They recorded their first single in 1963 and made it to number 25 on the British pop charts. Their later releases rose much higher on the charts, and their popularity soared.

Even as The Hollies enjoyed their successes, Nash's own sounds and interests were evolving. He was moving away from rock and pop and toward the new folk sounds emerging in the United States in the late 1960s. Nash began collaborating with David Crosby and Stephen Stills, whose music and political views meshed well with his own. In 1968 Nash left The Hollies to form Crosby, Stills & Nash.

CSN won the Grammy for best new artist in 1969. Joined off and on by Neil Young, the singers became an international superstar act known for strong harmonies and issue-driven lyrics.

In August 1969 the group played its second public show at the Woodstock music festival in New York. The experience did not start well for the band, whose helicopter nearly crashed on landing. Shaken but unhurt, Nash and his partners took the stage to perform for 400,000 dancing listeners.

Though they disbanded in 1971 to pursue solo careers, Crosby, Stills, and Nash—plus Young—still reunite to tour and record. In 1997 CSN was inducted into the Rock and Roll Hall of Fame. In 2009 they were inducted into the Songwriters Hall of Fame. And in 2010 The Hollies made it to the Rock and Roll Hall of Fame.

Nash has recorded five solo albums and 10 with CSN. He learned most of what he knows about singing and songwriting by doing it. In his early years, he imitated his favorite singers, but he recommends a different approach for singers today:

"Sing along to the records of your favorite singers. Nothing can prepare you better," Nash says. "Once you know how to approximate their voices, then forget it all, and it will come out your way."

Ultimately, Nash says, successful singers are those who recognize their strengths and desires, who can recognize a fine song, and who are dedicated to singing with passion.

"You have to be convinced that what you have to offer is worth someone's time. Nothing can replace the act of making music constantly. If you start, you can only get better at your craft," he says.

"Confidence and humor are the tools you need. Be sure that you want to be there, and go for it. Do everything while listening to your heart. You are the one that knows best."

Chapter 4

Singing, Off the Charts

You have the voice, the tools, and the determination to be a singer. You also have a long road ahead. Success is not easy to attain—or to keep.

Many popular young singers today have been packaged by producers and record labels. Their images and songs have been carefully crafted to sell merchandise and to bring screaming young fans to concerts. That level of success is difficult to achieve without the backing of a major music label. And even those singers often rise and fall quickly.

Many colleges and universities offer degrees in vocal performance.

Most singers never make the charts or have best-selling hits, but that does not mean they are not successful. Aspiring singers need to think beyond the stage and the recording studio.

A college degree is an important step. You can major in music, theater, dance, or other performing arts at many colleges and universities. It also is a good idea to think about getting another kind of degree to help you find jobs while you pursue your love of singing. After all, you will need to pay the rent while you audition for singing jobs. Some singers earn degrees in both music and a field such as teaching or business.

Visualize what you want to do with your voice. Think about how to turn your dreams into a career that might not be in the spotlight. Here are some ideas:

Some singers also work as recording engineers.

> » Record commercial jingles.
> » Teach music in schools.
> » Create community theater productions.
> » Become a lyricist, music writer, or music critic.
> » Become a music director, arranger, or producer.
> » Become a therapist who helps people strengthen their voices after surgery. Therapists also use music to help disabled people communicate and to comfort the ill.

If you are determined to stick with the stage or recording industry, think about starting as a background vocalist. You can get jobs with studios that need a pool of background singers, go on the road with artists, or work in theaters. Be prepared to start small. Sing in coffeehouses, bookstores, and libraries. Perform at festivals and community events. You may not be paid at first, but all experience is valuable.

Find a job at a recording studio or radio station to learn about the business. Create a sample CD and a résumé so you are ready when opportunity arises.

Expect to work your way up and to work hard. The journey may be slow and is likely to be discouraging at times, but keep going. Sing your heart out, and your story will be heard.

Get experience wherever you can. Renaissance festivals, for example, often hire costumed singers.

John Tartaglia
Singing Puppeteer

John Tartaglia has been performing for anyone who would listen since he was 3 years old. When Tartaglia was born in Maple Shade, New Jersey, in 1978, music already ran in his family. His mother is an actress and singer. His father is a composer, music director, and pianist. And his grandmother was an opera singer and a clown. No one was surprised when Tartaglia fell in love with puppets while watching *Fraggle Rock*, a television show by Muppets creator Jim Henson.

"I remember being fascinated by the emotional performances these amazing puppeteers got out of these simple puppets. I wanted to do what they were doing," Tartaglia says. "Singing as a puppet is honestly just like singing as a human."

Tartaglia began to sing and act in school and community theater. He took some formal lessons, though he credits his high school drama teacher and his mother with teaching him most of what he learned.

It was Tartaglia's own initiative, however, that launched his career as a singing puppeteer. When he was 12, he wrote a letter to Henson. He received an autographed photo and a letter from Henson's secretary. Henson died not long after.

Two years later Tartaglia wrote to another puppeteer, Kevin Clash, the man behind *Sesame Street*'s Elmo. Clash responded. He remembered Henson's talking about Tartaglia, and Clash asked him to send in tapes of his work. After attending a few workshops and auditions, Tartaglia began to work with the Muppets. At age 16 he started working on *Sesame Street*. He has played Elmo, Ernie, and many other characters on the show and in other Muppet productions.

In 2004 Tartaglia's *Sesame Street* connections carried him to Broadway, where he joined the cast of *Avenue Q* to create and perform the roles of Princeton and Rod. His

Avenue Q is very popular with audiences around the country.

performance earned him a 2004 Tony Award nomination for best actor in a musical.

After his success with *Avenue Q*, Tartaglia continued on Broadway, playing Lumiere in *Beauty and the Beast* and Pinocchio in *Shrek the Musical*.

In 2007 Tartaglia created and produced a TV show called *Johnny and the Sprites*, which ran worldwide for two seasons on *Playhouse Disney*. Today, while continuing both his

Broadway and Muppet work, Tartaglia is working on new television projects.

Tartaglia knows what it is like to start singing professionally at a young age. One of the biggest mistakes young singers make, he cautions, is trying to sound too much like their favorite stars. Tartaglia says he still has to be careful to trust his own style and instincts.

"The most successful people are the ones who know who they are and what they have to offer," he says. "Trust that you're unique and special. Find out what you do best, and work hard to make *that* what you focus on."

"Singers must care for their voices. It is common for young singers to push too hard and ignore problem signs. They end up injuring their voices and damaging their career chances," Tartaglia says.

Young performers should read books, attend shows, listen to music, and use the Internet to learn as much about their craft as possible.

"Listen, listen, listen!" Tartaglia says. "Success is unique to each performer. To me, success is having achieved whatever dream you have, no matter how big or small or crazy it may be. Success is as unique as dreams are."

BEING A GOOD SINGER ENOUGH IN TODAY'S MARKET?

To make music your career, you must understand what it takes to compete as a singer. Singer/songwriter Amy Otey shares some advice about becoming a singer.

1. UNDERSTAND HOW SONGS WORK

A singer must understand song structure—the mix of words and music. Words and music are arranged into sections: chorus, verse, and bridge. The music sets the mood. The words express emotion or meaning.

Analyze your favorite song. Why do you like it? What makes it different from songs you do not enjoy? Can you identify its parts and feel its rhythm?

Listen to as many songs as you can, and learn to hear the structure. Practice creative writing, read poetry, and learn the basics of rhyme to make you a better wordsmith.

2. DEVELOP GOOD STAGE PRESENCE

Practice standing and moving on stage. Learn to effortlessly hold a microphone. Find the spot to hold it so you sound your best. It is better to be too soft than too loud. Sound techs can turn up amplifiers, but if you are too loud, they cannot fix it. Learn how to set up and work your sound system, so you understand how it enhances your voice.

Stage presence can only be learned by being on stage—so get out there and sing!

Never say anything negative about yourself or other performers in front of an audience member.

Examine your performances to see how you can improve. Keep a journal of what does and does not work on stage. Use audience feedback, positive or negative, to improve.

Sing in front of an audience as much as you can. The more you do it, the more comfortable you will be. The more comfortable you are, the more fun you will have—and so will your audience.

3. LEARN THE BUSINESS

Think about how you want an audience to see you. Do not post silly or insulting pictures or comments about yourself or others online, especially in public forums like Facebook and MySpace. What you post online stays there forever. Negative information can hurt you later.

Learn about copyrights. Make sure you are allowed to perform another artist's songs in public. If you write a song, learn how to copyright it. Learn how to read a business contract.

Find out about organizations for singers in your town. For example, the National Association of Recording Artists and Songwriters has chapters around the country and runs a Student University. Ask whether you can join, or find out whether you can attend functions as a nonmember. You will learn about the music industry and meet people who can help you.

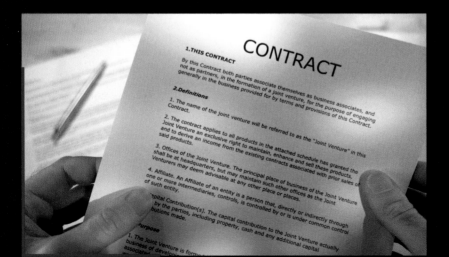

Having an image that matches your music is an important part of being marketable as a singer.

4. DEFINE YOUR IMAGE

Figure out what kind of singer you are and what you represent. Look at famous singers to see how they developed and redeveloped their images, goals, and music as they got older. Good case studies include Justin Timberlake, the Jonas Brothers, the Hansen Brothers, Stevie Wonder, Dolly Parton, and Loretta Lynn. Use their successes and mistakes to guide your path.

GLOSSARY

bridge one-time change in music (with or without lyrics), when the melody changes in rhythm or scale for a brief time, and then returns to the original tune

chorus lyrics and melody that repeat with little change; often the catchiest part of the song

diaphragm muscle tissue that separates the abdomen and chest cavities; the main muscle used in breathing

diva person who has difficulty working as part of a team

enunciation full and clear pronunciation of words

esophagus tube that carries food from the throat to the stomach

larynx upper part of the windpipe; the larynx holds the vocal cords

music theory study of the elements of music, including sound, rhythm, melody, and harmony

register term used to describe how the voice changes as it resonates in various parts of the body; singing voices usually are categorized into three registers: chest voice, middle voice, and head voice

resonates becomes louder and richer sounding

résumé brief list of a person's jobs, education, and awards

scale grouping of musical notes in ascending or descending order; Western music scales generally include 12 notes

song structure arrangement of words and music in a song, usually divided into sections called chorus, verse, and bridge

tempo speed of a song

verse unchanging melody with lyrics that change to tell the story of the song

READ MORE

Landau, Elaine. *Is Singing for You?* Minneapolis: Lerner Publications, 2011.

Marcovitz, Hal. *Carrie Underwood.* Broomhall, Pa.: Mason Crest, 2010.

Mattern, Joanne. *The Jonas Brothers.* Hockessin, Del.: Mitchell Lane Publishers, 2009.

Storey, Rita. *The Voice and Singing.* Mankato, Minn.: Smart Apple Media, 2010.

INTERNET SITES

FactHound offers a safe, fun way to find Internet sites related to this book. All of the sites on FactHound have been researched by our staff.

Here's all you do:

Visit *www.facthound.com*

Type in this code: 9780756543624

INDEX

About the Author

Rebecca Love Fishkin has written for newspapers, magazines, and Web sites, as well as books for young readers. She has managed an early literacy program and worked in the communications department of an international nonprofit organization that repairs children's cleft lips and palates. She lives in Lawrenceville, New Jersey.